Camp Wild

Orca currents

Pam Withers

ORCA BOOK PUBLISHERS

National Library of Canada Cataloguing in Publication Data

Withers, Pam
Camp Wild / Pam Withers.

(Orca currents)
ISBN 1-55143-361-3

I. Title. II. Series.

PS8595.I8453C34 2005   jC813'.6   C2005-900787-7

Summary: Wilf figures he's too old for summer camp
but has just what it takes to plot his escape from one.

First published in the United States, 2005
Library of Congress Control Number: 2005921298

Orca Book Publishers gratefully acknowledges the support for its publishing
programs provided by the following agencies: the Government of Canada
through the Book Publishing Industry Development Program (BPIDP), the
Canada Council for the Arts, and the British Columbia Arts Council.

Cover design: Lynn O'Rourke
Cover photography: Getty Images

Orca Book Publishers
PO Box 5626, Stn. B
Victoria, BC Canada
V8R 6S4

Orca Book Publishers
PO Box 468
Custer, WA USA
98240-0468

Printed and bound in Canada.
Printed on 30% post-consumer recycled paper,
processed chlorine-free using vegetable, low VOC inks.

08 07 06 05 • 5 4 3 2 1

For Lucille Dougherty

chapter one

"Summer camp!" I roar at my startled parents. Anger surges through my cracked voice with such electricity that I don't even blush about the vocal-chord break. "Why don't you just send me to Siberia? If you're so set on always getting rid of me, why did you even have a kid?"

That is going too far, I know the instant I've said it. But I'm livid they'd dare to mess with my summer plans without even asking me. A moment ago, they looked so pleased with themselves for having arranged it all. Then they looked surprised at my ungratefulness. And now they are both wearing a wounded expression.

"But you've always enjoyed Camp Wild," my mother protests.

I groan. How clued out can she be?

"Yeah, when I was eight," I blast back. "I'm fourteen now. Way too old for that crap. I told you last year I'd had it with that place."

My parents exchange a look. That is never a good sign.

"Wilf," my dad begins sternly, rubbing his freshly trimmed sideburns and tugging on his tie, which he hasn't removed even though he has been home from work for an hour. "You know as well as I do that we can't let you spend the entire summer on your own. You know your mother and I work long hours. You'll appreciate the structure and opportunities. You may be among the oldest campers this year, but that can't be all bad. Next year you can apply to be a junior camp counselor."

"Oh, that's rich, Dad," I explode back. "My dream job, looking after a bunch of brats. That would be even worse than being the only fourteen-year-old at a little-kids' summer camp. Don't do this, Mom and Dad. You can't make me go when you didn't even ask me first."

I shoot a sideways glance at my mother, at the beads of sweat beneath her pearl necklace. This exchange is getting to her, but Dad has that set jaw that makes me fear they really are going to go through with this.

"After what happened last month, son, we felt we didn't have a choice," he declares in his bank-executive voice, as though he is talking to a failed business owner looking for a loan. "You're too old for a baby-sitter and clearly not responsible enough to be unsupervised. We felt this was the best option. The subject is now closed." He loosens his tie as if that will force me to cave in.

I jump up and run out the door, my temper about to explode. I know what Dad is referring to, all right, but he never sees the whole picture. So I held a party at our house when he and Mom were working late one night. So what? A guy has to do something when left alone day and night by parents who are addicted to insane workloads. It wasn't my fault that a few uninvited thugs showed up and trashed the place a little. But I cleaned up the house. I endured the lectures. I even put up with being grounded for a month. Not that *being* grounded was much different from *not being* grounded. It's not like either of my parents cut back on their work to do stuff with me then. No, they just *phoned* me to make sure I was in my prison alone. They had clients to tend to, important clients. Always more important than me.

"Clients pay the bills," Dad is always saying cheerfully. Like my parents aren't so loaded that they can't pay for anything they want, including a little unexpected house-party damage, after-school lessons or summer camps to get rid of me so they can tend to more clients. Getting rid of me is always the point. Well, they are going too far this time. I am going to have a good summer, and it won't affect their clients one bit. They'll see me getting on the camp bus, all right, if that's all they care about. But the minute I get to Camp Wild, I'll be plotting my escape. I'll design my own summer adventure. I'll do an instant graduation from Camp Wild to Camp Wilf.

chapter two

The stupid bus ride was three hours long. And that was just the *first* bus ride. I was never so bored in my life. I had nothing to stare at but my new compass, because books and me and moving vehicles don't exactly go together. And Camp Wild, being a Nazi type of establishment, bans CD players, handheld video games and anything else that would've made the bus ride tolerable. I have to admit that the new compass is cool, though. A present from Mom and Dad just before my bus pulled up. They were obviously feeling guilty about forcing me to go to camp, but they couldn't exactly admit that at such a late stage, could they? So they gave me a compass. Yeah, guilt is good. Very good if it gets you something slick. I said all the right thank-yous and I'll-miss-you stuff, of course. Played the obedient, appreciative son to the hilt; I ought to be in the movies, in fact. Wouldn't they like to know what I'm really going to use this compass for? Won't they think twice about dumping me off next summer after they get a phone call from Camp Wild next week?

Anyway, here I am, standing where I was dropped off, thinking, after three hours on a bus, who needs a second bus ride? Okay, so it's a 4x4, not a bus, and it has "Camp Wild" marked on the side, and it's coming toward me across the parking lot this very minute. But in the end, it's another boring ride to take me to a boring camp.

"Hi! It's Wilf, right?" The muscle-bound guy driving puts the truck in neutral and jumps out to shake my hand. "I'm Patrick. Remember me?"

Yeah, I remember him from last year, sort of. Even though he mostly looked after the little kids.

"Yup," I say aloud, but I'm busy sneaking a peek at the girl getting out of the front passenger seat. Okay, so "peek" isn't the right word. I kind of have to force my eyes to the ground so as not to burn holes in her pretty body. I feel like a stick of butter melting in the sunshine.

"Hi, Wilf. I'm Claire," she says, walking toward us. She is smiling and holding out her hand. Like an idiot, I hand her my bag instead of squeezing that delicate palm and meeting her hazel eyes.

She giggles and tosses the bag into the truck as if its sixty pounds is no more than ten.

I cough. "Sorry, I could've... Um, are you a camper?"

It's not what I meant to say, but she does a tinkling laugh and moves away from Patrick, whose eyes are roaming the parking lot in search of more Camp Wild victims.

"I was last year but not during the same part of the summer as you, I guess. This year I'm a junior counselor. You can make that switch next year if you want. This is your last year as a camper, right?"

"Uh huh." Suddenly I feel like a little kid.

"That has to be Herb," Patrick shouts as he gallops over to a couple hugging a boy goodbye.

"Herb Green," Claire says, nodding toward the trio. "A first-timer at Camp Wild and a senior camper like you. In fact, the two of you are the only seniors this year. You are also cabin mates, so we'd better go meet him."

I pull my eyes off Claire long enough to survey a totally geeky boy wriggling away from his parents' smothering hugs. Poor kid. His parents are sniffling and making a scene. You'd think they were sending him off to the army during wartime. But he manages to escape them and walk hesitantly toward Claire and me as Patrick steps in to do the parental-reassurance thing.

"Hi, I'm Herb. A pleasure to meet you," Herb addresses us, blinking stupidly and shuffling his brand-new white tennis shoes, complete with Velcro tabs. His round face and innocent expression make him a candidate for a Boy Scouts poster. He holds his slightly lumpy body as awkwardly as a heron emerging from an oil slick. Adventurous this guy is definitely not, I decide.

"Hey, Herb," Claire addresses him. "I'm Claire, a junior counselor, and this is your cabin mate, Wilf, who has been attending Camp Wild since he was seven years old."

Great, she knows my whole life's story, and now Herb thinks I'm a Camp Wild groupie or something.

"Really?" Herb's eyes light up, and he looks me over like a little kid who has just met his hero. I avert my eyes from his Mickey Mouse watch. "You're so lucky. It's taken me a couple of years to get my parents to believe I can handle being away from them for two weeks." Then he blushes and drops his gear bag, which reads "City Bowling League." Eight (I repeat, *eight*) books spill out. *War and Peace* is on top. Is this guy for real?

"I'm so glad there's another camper my age," he rambles on. "And someone to share a cabin with." He's blinking again. "I've never camped before, so I kind of need someone to show me the ropes."

Ropes, eh? I picture myself handing him a rope shaped like a noose. I'm really not that nasty; I swear. I can't help it if a picture like that drops into my mind from out of nowhere. But how did I get the King of Nerds as a cabin mate? And we're the only seniors. Oh well. All the more reason to exit stage left as soon as I can. Let the little kids show Herb Green the ropes. He'll fit right in with them.

Claire leans down to pick up Herb's bowling bag and hoists it into the truck, then gives Patrick a thumbs-up. Unbelievable. She's strong, she's cute and she's only a year older. Too bad I'll be outta here before she can decide if she likes younger guys. *Dream on, Wilf. She's a baby-sitter. And you're one of the babies.*

"Two to pick up, and two now collected," Patrick announces. "Jump in,

Herb and Wilf. We're off to do wild things at Camp Wild."

My sarcasm detector detects none. My respect for Patrick drops like a boulder off a cliff. Is Claire in training to become a brainwashed tool of the regime too? Maybe I can save her from her fate, whisk her off the grounds before it's too late. I flash my best bus-station grin at my three truck mates. Then I sigh and nod graciously at Herb the Greenie, my soon-to-be ex-cabin mate.

chapter three

The kids press around me wide-eyed as I strike the match. Slowly, carefully, I bring the flame close to my upper left leg, just below my shorts. I smile as I apply it to the black backside of the tick that has dared to bury its head in my leg. The kids "ooh" and "ahh" as some leg hairs singe. I'm concentrating so hard that I barely notice the obnoxious smell of burning hair.

"Look! It's working!" shouts a little brat called Charlie Carson.

"Of course it's working," I pronounce as the tick withdraws its head in a hurry. "They don't like lit matches on their butts while they're feeding. You either smother 'em with Vaseline or touch 'em with a match to get 'em to back out."

"Why not just pull them out?" Charlie asks.

"Because the head usually breaks off and stays in," Claire begins.

"And then you might get an infection," Patrick finishes.

I pick up my half-fried assailant, show him around the little crowd as they chant "yuck," then toss him at Charlie.

"Hey," Claire chastises me as the other kids giggle and clear away, but Charlie, scoundrel that he is, catches the little bug and starts chasing some girls with it. He holds the tick high above his spikes of dirty red hair and waves it like a trophy.

There's no putting off that little horror, who has been following me around every moment he can. He's like an embedded tick himself, I reflect, but seniors aren't allowed to apply matches to the behinds of first-year harassers.

I sneak a smile at Claire and retreat toward my cabin. Claire and Patrick round everyone back to their cabins for "quiet time."

"Can't believe we've been here only two days," I say to Herb as I leap up the steps to our cabin just ahead of him. I throw myself down on my narrow lower bunk, which I claimed the first day. "Feels like two weeks already."

"Nah, feels like two days," he replies, scraping his shoes on the doormat outside for a full two minutes before opening the screen door. "That was really brave of you," he adds. "I'd freak if I got a tick."

"Yeah? Well you probably will, and it's no biggie."

"Well, other than ticks, isn't this place the greatest?" he says. "Everyone is so nice. I'm having a great time. I even like the food. What's your favorite activity, Wilf? Mine's canoeing."

"My favorite activity is quiet time," I declare, hoping he'll take the hint. I pull the *Sports Illustrated* swimsuit issue from under my pillow and turn toward the wall, willing him to find another victim for his happy-talk. To my amazement, he crawls up the bunk ladder in his unsteady way and tucks into *War and Peace*.

My little notebook falls out from the pages of my magazine. I study it carefully. It holds my top-secret strategies in code. Looking it over, I figure just two more days before I pull off my sneak departure. I've been plotting like crazy. By day I go through the motions of a good camper; by night I polish my plans. My days go something like this: First, breakfast in the log dining lodge under the mounted moose antlers, where my motor-mouth cabin mate follows me around like a boom box that I've forgotten to unstrap from my shoulder. Next, archery class, where I am useless. Then, arts and crafts (give me a break), wilderness survival, first aid (I'm all ears in those sessions), sailing (maybe the knot-tying stuff will come in handy), and canoeing and kayaking. Now, canoeing and kayaking is where I've always excelled and where I'm hoping to put the finishing touches on my plot. Somehow, I have to find out what's downstream. Downstream, I'm hoping, is my ticket out of this fun-park.

The biggest surprise about our canoeing and kayaking class is that Herb has actually been in canoes before. In fact, I'd say he's been in them a lot. I guess his overprotective parents must have decided at some point that he was okay in canoes if he was within arm's reach. Like a sea lion, he's awkward as heck on land but astonishingly strong and smooth the minute he hits water.

After canoeing and kayaking class comes lunch, where my main project is spiriting away as many cans of food as will fit up my sleeves, down my shorts or under my baseball cap. The trick is getting stuff out without a soul seeing me. This, as it turns out, is where I truly excel. Although I don't expect to be around for Camp Wild's last-day awards ceremony, I reckon I'd ace the blue ribbon for food-supplies diversion if I were.

Afternoons mean tennis (yawn), swimming (Claire in a bikini: wow!), and free time (during which I stash stolen food beneath the cabin's floorboards while Herb is out). Then there's supper (more supplies to collect), campfire singing, and "lights out." (I did mention that Nazis run this camp, didn't I?)

A loud crunching noise above me interrupts my thoughts.

"Hey, we're not supposed to eat in the cabin. It attracts rodents," I quote Patrick as I watch pieces of potato chip fall past me.

"Oh, you want some?" Herb's ugly, upside-down face appears above me.

When I don't reply, he says, "Wilf, what are you writing in that little note-book of yours? How come you won't tell me? You're always writing stuff down."

"I'm recording everything you eat, Herb. I'm an undercover junk-food policeman."

"Hey, I need the energy for afternoon classes. And for getting away from Charlie. He follows you around too, doesn't he? Is he really only ten?"

"So they say. I consider him the king of hyperactivity and the prince of deviousness. But he can paddle a kayak like a demon."

"That's 'cause his dad taught him. And he likes you, Wilf. You have noticed he likes you, right?"

"Herb, I'm only going to say this once. I hate kids. And on the brat scale of one to ten, Charlie rates an eleven."

Herb laughs. "Yeah? Well he worships the ground you walk on."

And sticks to me worse than you, I think. Did I ask for two demented shadows?

"I'm going for a walk," I say aloud.

"But it's quiet time."

"Exactly." I heave myself up, tuck my notebook into my back pocket and stride out the door. I let the screen door slam. I walk briskly to the canoe house and step inside. The moldy smell of drying lifejackets assaults my nose. I scan the racks and stick my head inside the shortest aluminum canoe to inspect it. Too long. Good thing I know where the shorter, solo canoes are stored. I select two paddles (one as a spare), a lifejacket and wetsuit just my size, a helmet, flotation bags, waterproof gear bags and a bailer. I glance around to make sure I'm alone, then stash them in a cobwebby corner beneath a tarp. I pull out my notebook and start checking things off.

"Hi, Wilf. Whatcha doin'?"

I swing around. His head is poking out from under the longest canoe, and he's grinning all over.

"Hey, Charlie. Just making sure all the gear's ready for class tomorrow. What are you doing here?"

His beady little eyes bore into me. He squeezes out from under the canoe and brushes dirt off his overalls. "Spying."

"Yeah? Well I wouldn't spy from under there. Probably mice or rats in this shed."

He grins wider. "You can't scare me."

It's too true. I pull a stick of gum from my shirt pocket and offer it to him. He grabs it, then tears out of the shed like I might change my mind.

"I hate kids," I mutter as I jam a stick of gum into my own mouth and head down to the river. "Especially that one."

chapter four

"Wilf, Herb, wake up guys."

Patrick's voice wafts through our cabin's screen door, but I know for a fact it's not seven o'clock yet. How do I know? Because the camp's obnoxious wake-up bugle hasn't blasted through the chill morning air. And the sun hasn't yet cast beams of light on the clothes Herb and I have left scattered about our tiny cabin. (That's the only thing we have in common, I've decided.)

"Go away," I mumble, and sink deeper into my sleeping bag.

Patrick takes this as an invitation to step in.

"Sorry you two, but one of our canoe and kayak instructors is ill this morning. I'd normally take over for him, but I have to run into town on business. I'm wondering if you can help out. Just one class: the little kids."

"No thanks," I say.

"You bet!" Herb pronounces at the same time. I feel the entire bunk bed sway as he sits up above me.

I lift my feet and push up on the mattress beneath him in the hope he'll take it back. But he's such a suck-up to Patrick, I know he won't.

"Ow! Wilf, stop doing that. You heard Patrick. He needs help."

"Wilf, are you in?" Patrick's voice sounds a little muffled from inside my sleeping-bag cocoon. "I've noticed you're both strong paddlers. Claire would really appreciate your help."

Claire? I pop my head out of its shell. As it turns out, I'm suddenly *sooo* available to help juniors with their J-strokes. "Sure, why not? Does that get us out of arts and crafts?"

"If you like," Patrick says. "Thanks, guys. It'll be good training if you want to be junior counselors next year, you know." The screen door slams, the bugle sounds, the sun creeps in to expose our messy cabin.

"Like we want to be junior counselors," I gripe. I crawl out of bed and splash water on my face from the dirty washbowl I was supposed to empty last night.

"Wilf, you'd make an awesome one if you wanted to be. You know exactly how the camp runs, and the kids love you."

The kids love me? "Like cats who jump on the laps of people allergic to cats."

"Yeah, well the kids never talk to *me*."

"Maybe if you talked *at* them less, Herbie."

"Wilf, why are you always so negative? This place is a blast. Relax and enjoy it. It'll be fun teaching this afternoon. Bet the cook will even give us extra portions at supper."

Ah, a second thing we have in common. A desire for more food than we're allotted. But my agenda is long-term and more noble. Well, okay, maybe not so noble.

The morning drags by. Finally it's the kiddies' canoe and kayak class. Claire's on the shore fitting out the munchkins in puffy orange lifejackets. I admire her pierced navel from afar, not for the first time.

"Wilf, Herb! Thanks guys, for being willing to help out," she calls. As we come close, she adds in a lowered voice, "This group can be a handful for just one person."

"Aw, they're just normal kids with good energy," I say smoothly as I help her lift some kayaks from the upper racks of the boat shed. Herb's eyebrows slant in confusion at my remark before he shakes his head and starts rummaging around the rack of paddles.

"Charlie, can you help me carry these?" I hear him shout.

"Nah, I'm gonna help Wilf," he says, appearing beside me. For a split second, I feel the throb of where I extracted that tick yesterday.

"Charlie, dude, let's see if you can carry more paddles than Herb and I can," I say.

He eyes me carefully, then falls for it. Competitive little devil, I think. Soon we have seven little water rats on the river, four in canoes and the rest in kayaks.

"Everyone switches boats in half an hour so we all learn both types of paddling," Claire reminds them.

"Not me," declares Charlie. "I only want to kayak." Claire ignores him.

I dig my knees into my canoe's foam kneepads and demonstrate the art of crossing the river's mild current, as Claire in her kayak and Herb in his canoe do the same. One by one, our little ducklings imitate our best forward, back and sweep strokes, crossing and re-crossing the river. The canoeists demonstrate their J and crossbow strokes as well, some a little shakily. Now and then, a student gets washed downstream, prompting Claire and Herb to give chase and coax the kid back up the eddies. Once, a timid girl capsizes in her kayak, ejects and comes to the surface gasping.

"You should of rolled," Charlie chastises her from his bright orange kayak.

"Now, Charlie, you know you're the only one in this group who knows how to roll," Claire says.

"You can roll?" I ask, surprised.

In response, the ten-year-old makes sure I'm watching before capsizing and righting his kayak three times in a row.

"Show-off," his wet classmate mumbles as she eases herself back into her kayak.

"Awesome, buddy," I say to Charlie with a thumbs-up, only because it makes Claire smile warmly at me. "That'll come in real handy when you do rapids. Speaking of which, Claire, what's downstream of here?" I remember talk from past summers about wild whitewater, but I never registered the details.

Claire smiles indulgently, allows the kids to paddle into a sort of huddle in the biggest eddy and stabs her paddle in the direction I'm looking.

"It's nice, gentle-flowing water for about half an hour, which is what makes this site such a safe place to learn. Then the river starts dropping faster and becomes rapids with boulders the size of cars that you have to maneuver around."

"Cool," Charlie inserts, but some of the tykes are clutching their paddles and looking behind them nervously.

"And then?" prompts Herb.

"Then it drops into a narrow canyon with steep walls on both sides and non-stop rapids for hours. It's really, really intense."

"You've canoed it?" the little girl with wet hair asks, wide-eyed.

"I have," Claire says solemnly, staring at the dark water beside her canoe as if it's replaying the footage. "I did it with a bunch of crazy guys last summer. I'd never do it again."

"Why?" the kids shout together as they inch closer to her, the same way they do when she tells ghost stories around the evening campfire.

Claire's eyes glow with a faraway look. "Because there's a killer waterfall at the end of the canyon, and you have only seconds to get out before you reach it. Plus you need ropes to climb down from there to the last rapids before the river dumps into a wilderness lake. It's not safe, and we should never have done it," she says solemnly.

I mentally add rope to my equipment list. I want to ask about those last rapids before the lake, but I don't want to make her suspicious. So I turn to order the kids back to their paddling exercises. Claire tosses me a grateful look. One by one, our charges return to paddling Camp Wild's decidedly un-wild river bend. All except Charlie, whose eyes, squinting beneath the wet spikes of red hair sticking through his kayak helmet's drain holes, refuse to leave my face.

chapter five

Today is D-Day, as in time to defect from this camp. That puts me in such a generous mood that at the breakfast buffet, I load one Danish into my mouth, two more into my pockets and deliver a fourth to Herb. He is hunched on the bench that pulls up to the long mess-hall table.

"Herbie, buddy, extra rations for you," I say cheerfully, dropping it on his plate.

"No thanks," he says glumly, stirring a spoon listlessly in his oatmeal.

Wait a second. What's wrong with this picture? I'm the glum guy; he's always Mr. Happy.

"What's up? Got up on the wrong side of your bunk?" Not technically possible, but hey, I'm being real nice this morning 'cause in just hours I'll never share a bunk with him again.

"Got toilet-cleaning duty today, and Patrick won't let me trade. What'd you draw?"

"K.P. Want me to snitch some chocolate bars for you?" Getting kitchen patrol is like winning the lottery at Camp Wild. Even though it means scrubbing pots for an hour, it also means potential access to the pantry's box of chocolate bars. Never mind that Cook makes you whistle the whole time you are in the pantry. (That way you can't stuff anything in your mouth.) She also checks your pockets when you come out. But the best-informed campers know she does not check socks or hats.

Toilet-cleaning duty, on the other hand, is losing the lottery. Poor old Herb. I watch him frown and shake his head.

"Flag time," Patrick announces in his booming voice as he stands at the front of the room. I silently order the moose antlers on the wall above him to fall on his skull, but they don't cooperate. So I file out behind Herb to where two juniors are proudly unfolding the flag and getting ready to run it up the pole. Did I do stupid stuff like this a few years ago? Do my parents really think I am still a kid? Are their careers really so much more interesting than their own offspring?

I try to regain my cheerfulness by reminding myself that tonight, the minute Herb starts snoring, I'll be turning tail on this poor excuse for a daycare center. I can paddle down to the rapids by moonlight, hide in the woods till dawn and be into the canyon before tomorrow's bugle blows. I'm figuring on a waterfall portage by sundown tomorrow. After that, I'll set up my hideaway on the lake. I'll get fresh water from the creeks that run into it, and I'll make myself a nifty lean-to. The only classes I'll attend are sleeping in, sunbathing, swimming and fishing. Someone will find me eventually, of course, no matter how well I hide the canoe. But I'll have my fun until they do, and my parents will get the point. For a couple of days, maybe even longer, I'll be an explorer, Robinson Crusoe, Daniel Boone, whatever.

"Patrick has turned mean," Herb interrupts my daydream as flag time wraps up, and we drift back toward our cabin.

"Patrick, the guy you like so much?" I dig.

"Yeah, he made me spend an hour this morning cleaning up our cabin. Said we need to set a better example for the juniors."

"How come he didn't haul me in to help?"

"'Cause you'd snuck off somewhere, as usual. Then Cook caught me swiping a cinnamon bun before breakfast. For punishment, she made me wash dishes."

"This surprises you?"

"I tried telling her that they don't give us enough food at this camp, and she calls Patrick in. He lectures me in front of all the little kids lined up for breakfast, and they start laughing and calling me fat. What a bunch of brats. They're all Patrick really cares about. It's no fun being the only seniors, is it?"

"You're being very negative about Camp Wild," I can't resist digging some more.

"And the classes are getting boring."

What? Is this Herb Green, my insufferable cabin mate, or has his evil double just walked onstage? I shrug and look at him more closely.

"Hey, let's skip out of archery and go skip rocks on the river," Herb suggests.

I'm shocked, awed, impressed. "Sure." I'm such a good-hearted guy that, half an hour later, I even let him win a couple of times. Never mind that I'm capable of launching pebbles that hovercraft all the way to the other side of the river.

"I don't want to do toilet cleaning. Why should we have to do chores when we pay for the rotten experience of being stuck here for two weeks? This place sucks."

Whoa. Boy Scout poster-boy has turned in his badge. I'm amused. "So what was your first clue?"

"Look, I know you don't like me, Wilf, but you know I can canoe. In fact, I've had way more whitewater experience than you, so you need me if you're heading downriver to get away from this place. Let me go with you."

My jaw feels like a support piece has just fallen out. "What're you talking about, Herb?"

"The big food stash under the floorboards in our cabin. The little notebook with a list of all the supplies you've been stealing or hiding. And especially the canoe and paddle you've stashed in the bushes downstream of camp."

I rub my chin, struggling to come up with a clever response. Sadly, I produce nothing but silence and sweat.

"You hate the place, and you've been planning an escape for days. I'm not as dumb as you think, Wilf. I can report this to Patrick and Claire, or you can take me with you. Choose wisely, cabin mate." He turns and studies me, evil eyes unblinking.

"I don't have enough food for two." I say. I feel panic start to set in.

"You're on K.P. today. That'll make it easy, Wilf. Anyway, between us, we'll have plenty by tomorrow. And from what Claire said, no one would dare follow us downstream. They'll probably drive to that lake and paddle across it, hoping to catch us there. We can be hiding in the woods by then. I suggest leaving tomorrow night."

A turkey vulture's squawk from a branch above startles me. Is it laughing at me or signaling that someone may be eavesdropping nearby? I survey the woods around us and satisfy myself that we're otherwise alone. I feel like a cornered animal, but I'm working it all out fast. He can canoe. I have K.P. today. Tomorrow night is only one day past a full moon. Most importantly, I can ditch him after we've escaped. To do that, though, I'll need to persuade him to paddle his own canoe. I nod slowly, extend a hand to Herb. We shake hands. He follows me to a shed near the canoe house.

"Last year, the camp bought a bunch of new double canoes," I tell him. "To make room for them in the boathouse, they dumped a couple of the oldest solos in this shed. It's locked, but there's a hole in the back wall we can fit through. The hole's big enough to get the canoes out too. That's how I got the canoe I've hidden. It'll take them longer to notice two stolen singles from here than a double from the boathouse. Are you okay with that?"

"Sure, I like paddling solo," Herb says.

"Don't forget to grab a wetsuit, helmet and two paddles," I say as we climb through the hole. "A spare paddle is important."

chapter six

"Charlie, you're coming out of the eddy at nine o'clock. I said eleven o'clock, or you won't get across the river without getting swept down."

I'm referring, of course, not to the time, but the angle of his kayak bow as it crosses the upstream/downstream line of current just off shore. Luckily, he's a smart kid (not just a smart-ass kid). He adjusts his eddy exit technique and works his little biceps on the sweep stroke till he's sitting pretty on the far side of the river.

"Nice going, buddy," Claire calls out approvingly. "See, everyone? That was a perfect example of a ferry. Who's next?"

Herb and I glance at our watches. We're being model campers and class helpers today, and why wouldn't we be, with only five hours to go before departure time?

"Charlie," I direct as he strokes the water impatiently across the river, waiting for another turn. "See that big flat rock in the middle of the river? I'm going to purposely brush its upstream side on the way over to you. I want you to watch how I lean hard downstream onto it to prevent my canoe from getting stuck against it or tipping. Remember, kids, how we talked about that safety maneuver? Charlie, try it after me to show the others how it works in a kayak, okay? We're all right here if you have problems."

That lights up his little face. The second I've finished my demonstration, he shoots out of his eddy like a torpedo. Of course, he leans downstream too early and flips over. But like a battery-operated toy, he rolls and pops back up almost faster than the water can get his face wet. His boat washes neatly around the rock. The kid is hot in a kayak, even if he can be really irritating.

"Good stuff, Charlie," Claire says. "Okay, kids. It's five o'clock. Quitting time." As the other juniors pump to shore, I watch Charlie work his way back upstream and attack the rock again. He gets it right this time. He's a determined little cuss.

As soon as Claire, Herb and I have made sure all the equipment is back on its racks, Claire turns and blocks our way out of the boathouse door.

"Guys, you've been a real help with the kids. The other instructor is back tomorrow, so you can go back to being just campers. But I really hope you decide to do the junior counselor thing next summer. You're both naturals."

"Thanks," Herb replies, blinking bigtime.

"You never know," I say, unable to meet those hazel eyes and long lashes. "It's been real, anyway." Like, *real tempting to ask you out and real humiliating being a camper.*

Five hours later, Herb and I pull on our wetsuits and pack the stuff we've filched from supper into a waterproof bag. I sling it over my shoulder as we slink out the cabin door. Everything's dark and quiet, save for where the moon shines. And the moon doesn't shine on the route we pick to our hidden canoes. Nor does the turkey vulture call out as two canoes slip silently into the inky water. With one last glance behind us, we whisper good riddance to the kiddie kingdom in the woods. Here we come, real adventure.

"Ever paddle by moonlight before?" Herb whispers fifteen minutes later, as we draw up beside one another in the gentle current.

"Nope. Have you?" I ask, one eye on the black water ahead.

"Yes, when my parents and I were late getting to our takeout point one day. It's fun when there are no rapids, at least until the moon goes behind a cloud."

I study the big white eye in the sky and notice how mottled its luminescent surface is. A cloud scuttles across its lower face, hiding what seems for a second like a smirk.

"You canoe a lot with your parents?"

"Since I was too young to remember," Herb replies. "But they never let me do any big whitewater. They're total control freaks and still treat me like I'm a kid."

"I know the feeling."

"Your parents are overprotective?"

"No, the opposite. They're always finding ways to get rid of me so they can fit in a few more hours of work. They haven't figured out that I've grown up while they've been busy being workaholics."

"So that's why you hate Camp Wild? 'Cause they dump you here?"

"Something like that."

"How often have you canoed river rapids?"

"Spent two intense weeks in a white-water canoeing course my parents signed me up for. I can handle the canyon coming up, if that's what you're asking." *I hope, anyway.*

We both jump as a splash sounds nearby. Herb flicks his flashlight on just in time to see a tail disappear.

"River otter," he observes. "Listen."

My ears perk up. I can hear fast moving water. I can feel the canoe picking up speed. I reach out, draw a wide sweep stroke and begin pumping for shore. Herb is several strokes ahead of me. Everything happens fast after that. A cloud blots out the moon. I hear Herb leap into the water and haul his boat up to shore with a giant heave. Then, just as I realize I've missed the last easy eddy to catch, I hear a splash and feel my canoe being hauled to safety by Herb's shadowy figure.

Okay, I take it back. He's not geeky and lumpy and useless. Well, he is, but not when there's a canoe in the vicinity. As we hide the canoes and bed down in the dark forest, I secretly decide not to ditch him till we're through the whitewater.

"Wilf?" he says as I'm drifting off to sleep.

"Yeah?"

"This is fun. I'm glad you decided to run away."

"Uh huh. Good night, Herb." Thankfully, no bunk bed shakes as he turns over and starts snoring.

chapter seven

"Herb, wake up." The dew is so heavy on his sleeping bag that my hand gets wet shaking him. He sits upright. His sleepy eyes take in the dawn. Mickey Mouse confirms that it's nearly six AM.

"Got to get into the canyon before anyone figures out we're gone," I urge. "I don't think they'll follow us past the canyon entrance."

"I agree," he says groggily.

We munch on some chocolate bars and drink heavily from our water bottles. We pack up our gear and stow it, carefully balanced, in our canoes. We've divided the food supplies between us in case one of us tips and loses his boat. I shiver in the weak morning light as I don my wetsuit and scout the first rapid. No big deal. Just a little maneuvering, I decide.

I lash the extra paddle in place and mutely apologize to Camp Wild for taking off with all this equipment. But hey, it'll all be back on the racks soon. Anyway, I'm a paying customer at the camp, just on a sort of "independent study program" at the moment.

Herb is coiling his rescue rope into its special bag and placing it within easy reach. I wanted to do this trip alone, but for the moment, I'm vaguely glad of his presence.

We push off and suddenly, I'm too busy to think of anything but how to keep my canoe upright and undented. River boulders start coming at us like a horizontal meteor shower. J-stroke, sweep, crossbow. Sweep, draw, breathe. For half an hour, we slalom through the rock gardens, too distracted to enjoy their beauty. There's an occasional bang or scrape in shallow stretches, but no one is getting stuck or tipped or panicked, yet. The rescue ropes lie unused. My confidence is building. This is the life, I decide, pitting oneself against nature. I watch the sun rise over three-storey trees. Down the shore, startled deer raise their antlered heads and bound away. A silver arch flashes ahead, a fish longer than my arm. Cool. An eagle's white plumage catches my eye as it tilts overhead like a small plane signaling hello.

Mom and Dad would enjoy this, I reflect. I've seen old photos of them canoeing lakes. I guess that was before I was born. Did having a child spoil everything for them? I picture my birth certificate being delivered to them with a telegram that states, *Kid, fun or work: Choose two of these three.* Reluctantly, they tick off *kid* and *work.* A few years later, after they have become successful, a second telegram demands, *Now choose one of the two.*

"Wilf!" Herb is still leading. Maybe I should take over, but hey, blackmailers don't deserve any favors. Let him be the first down the rapids, like a miner's canary.

"What?"

He points ahead. I follow his finger to the granite walls squeezing in. Yup. Our river is feeding us into a roofless tunnel, a gorge that dictates no chance of paddling or walking back upstream, let alone portaging anything tricky. This is a good thing, I remind myself. It makes us safe from pursuit until we hit the lake. At that point, anyone from camp wanting to catch us will be coming from the other direction. On this much Herb and I have agreed.

I glance behind and see nothing but rapids well conquered. I glance ahead and feel my breath catch. Our rock garden appears to be sliding downhill like an avalanche. The river is foaming, pitching and seething as if angry at being bottlenecked between sheer cliffs.

"Whoa," I tell my canoe. "Slow down." I don't think it can hear me, nor do I think it trusts me at the reins. It plunges into the white and starts bucking. I fasten my eyes on a big, calm eddy far below. I dig in and bite my tongue as I fight to reach it. How cold will this water be if I spill in, I wonder. I'm wearing a wetsuit, lifejacket and helmet, but they seem slim protection against what this river is becoming.

Claire said the canyon has rapids non-stop for hours. What chance do Herb and I have of arriving at the falls still in our boats? As I pry my way past a boulder the size of a bulldozer, I decide Clare wasn't exaggerating about this section being intense. But she and her buddies made it. Doesn't that mean Herb and I will?

At least it has a few big eddies where we can stop and catch our breath. We grab them the way trapeze artists leap from swing to swing. In these calm patches, we bail water out of our canoes with large cut-off plastic milk jugs, slow our breathing and crane our necks to scout what is coming up next. Once or twice during the first hour, we stop long enough to drink water and congratulate one another on our success so far.

"What's for lunch?" Herb asks during one such pause.

I dig through the tins and produce

two cans of tuna, a can opener and two plastic forks.

"Caught fresh this morning," I joke. Herb's mouth is already too full to answer.

Fifteen minutes later, I am watching a mother duck and her ducklings work their way upstream, wishing I had that kind of power in my paddle, when I hear a cry and catch a flash of orange in the whitewater above. Herb and I jump out of our canoes onto a large, flat rock beside us.

"No way," I mutter in disbelief. It's Charlie, bobbing behind an empty kayak. We quickly grab our rescue ropes and let fly. The ropes fall close enough to Charlie that he is able to grab them with his free hand. The other hand is applying a death grip to his paddle and stern's grab loop.

Good boy, I think. You remembered

to stay behind your kayak, keep your feet up and hold onto your paddle.

Good boy? More like, *What the heck are you doing here? And who else is coming down the river behind you?*

"S-s-sorry," Charlie splutters as Herb and I lift him from the water onto the rock. "I rolled three times, but I just c-c-couldn't on the last spill."

Herb and I look at one another. We shade our eyes to look upstream.

"Charlie, are you alone?" Herb asks.

"Yes," he says as defiantly as a semi-hypothermic ten-year-old can. He's shivering so hard that his teeth are rattling. I look at his blue hands.

"Out of that wetsuit, now," I order. Herb, obviously thinking along the same lines, pulls my sleeping bag from its waterproof bag in the canoe.

Charlie doesn't argue. He may be a sneak, a thief and a pain, and he may have just jinxed our getaway, but for now, he's a dangerously cold kid who needs serious warming up. He's also one heck of a gutsy and competent guy to have gotten this far.

chapter eight

It's the middle of the afternoon, and I'm peeling lumps of moss off our rock and hurling them into the river impatiently. Herb is babying Charlie, who is curled up in my sleeping bag on the flattest portion of our tiny island. He has stopped shivering. I figure he's nearly warmed up enough to carry on.

"Sure you don't need another snack?"

Herb asks Charlie. "We have chocolate bars, canned applesauce, even canned chili." *Yeah, thanks to me.*

"I'm okay," Charlie says in a low, flat voice.

"What about another sweater? I brought an extra one."

"I'm okay," he says sharply. The flash of defiance is a good sign.

"Whatever made you think you could kayak whitewater like this by yourself, kid?" Herb continues. "Couldn't you see how dangerous it was? What if we hadn't been here? You'd have died! Not to mention how upset you're making everyone back at camp. They know Wilf and I can cope. They'll go nuts knowing you've followed us. Or they'll think we had something to do with you disappearing."

Charlie stays silently curled up like a caterpillar on a leaf.

"Wilf, try and tell him how stupid and unsafe this was."

I shrug. "I never asked either of you to follow me. And I never fooled myself into thinking that it was smart or safe to canoe alone."

"Yeah, well here we are. None of us can paddle back upstream or climb these cliffs. So what're we going to do?"

I toss another lump of moss into the water. "I think you just answered that for yourself."

"Wilf, are you saying Charlie should carry on down with us? He's not good enough. His swim just proved that."

"I got down lots of rapids already," Charlie says, standing up. His eyes flash. "And I rolled three out of four times."

I reach into my canoe for my water-proof sack and toss it to Charlie. "Back in your wetsuit, Charlie. I don't care if you ride in Herb's canoe or if you kayak. I'm outta here."

Herb's mouth drops open a little, but Charlie knows I mean it. He's out of the sleeping bag and into his damp wetsuit and kayak fast. Within minutes, I'm leading, my rage fueling every stroke. Charlie is paddling like a madman to stay on my tail, and Herb is shouting at us to slow down. One big happy family. Every time we stop to rest, Herb's all over Charlie like a Papa Bear. "Are you okay? Need to rest? Tell me if you want to ditch the kayak and get in my canoe. You aren't shivering, are you?"

I say nothing. Half the time, I don't even warn them before I surge on ahead. Charlie's keeping up amazingly well. He capsizes and rolls once: a good, no-hesitation roll. The one time I see him nearly splat against a rock, he leans into it and pushes away, just like I taught him. He has no right to be with us, but he's surviving. He deserves to be scared out of his mind, but he shows no fear.

"Charlie, follow the deepest channel in this next rapid," Herb is shouting from the back. "Don't forget to accelerate in the big wave at the bottom and don't get sideways to it, okay? You're not afraid, are you? Watch out for logs, now."

I offer neither advice nor encouragement. As far as I'm concerned, it's every man for himself, and Charlie has opted for manhood. But now and then I wonder what keeps Charlie going: my cold silence and the fear of being left behind or a desire to keep out of earshot of Herb's nagging. If he or Herb tips into the river, I'll attempt a rescue, of course. Other than that, I haven't signed on to be anyone's lifeguard, friend or coach. This was supposed to be my big solo adventure, my proof that I could live in the wilds on my own. And the wilds are supposed to be quiet, not filled with Herb's frantic chatter.

Trouble is, Charlie's unexpected arrival and his close call with hypothermia have set us back a few hours. And even though

I'm not slowing down much for my two uninvited companions, I'm not going as fast as I would without them. I'd hoped to make the falls before dark. Now I'm not sure that's going to happen.

"Guys, don't forget to keep drinking water," Herb says as we complete a steep drop. "Otherwise we could get dehydrated. Wilf, better let me lead for awhile."

"No way."

"Why not? We're in this together. We need to change off, keep fresh. Anyway, you're not being thoughtful of Charlie. He's not as strong as us. We need to take more breaks."

"Shut it, Herb. Both of you are gate-crashers on my party. Don't be anchors too, or I'll cut the chain."

"Wilf, you're being ridiculous..."

And so on, as Charlie keeps tight-lipped and just keeps on paddling. In fact, in the milder rapids' playful waves,

I even detect a smile. He can surf, spin and catch up with us, even if we don't pause, because his kayak is so much lighter.

I'm selecting eddies I'm sure Charlie can catch. We all hop from one to the next, twisting and turning out of harm's way in between. Both roller coaster waves that hide what's coming next and rocks lurking just beneath the surface spell danger. As I complete one particularly hairy rapid successfully, I hear a shout behind me. I turn to see Herb's canoe thrown precariously against a tall boulder in the middle of the river. He has done the right thing: leaned hard into the rock, but he has lost his paddle in the process. As water pounds into the upstream side of Herb's canoe, I see the paddle disappear around the river bend below me. Do I chase it, or stand by ready to help? Herb is frantically trying to unleash his spare paddle without upsetting the boat.

Charlie enters my eddy safely, concern on his face.

I reach for my rescue rope, hoping I won't have to use it. Just as Herb frees his spare paddle, a surge of water slams the canoe even harder against the rock. The second paddle drops into the water and slides away as Herb only just manages to steady the now waterlogged boat. He's at severe risk of sinking and of his canoe wrapping like a dishcloth against the upstream side of the boulder. The boulder itself is too steep for him to climb up onto. In moments, he'll be in the icy water—or worse, trapped underwater against boat and rock.

I'm still trying to figure out what to do when Charlie sprints out of our eddy with a tidy eleven o'clock angle. He works his way against all odds to the middle of the river, just beneath Herb's boulder. Then, carrying on to where only a small kayak could maneuver, he reaches the floating spare paddle. He picks it up, makes his way back to below the boulder and throws it upriver to Herb.

Herb, looking relieved, catches it and bails like crazy with his chopped-down milk jug. As Charlie returns to my side, Herb tries a high-risk move. He leans hard against the boulder, and using his hands like claws against it—one still clutching the retrieved paddle—he pulls himself and his canoe past the rock. Then he uses his paddle to brace upright as he slides past his stony captor.

When he finally arrives in our eddy, I let my breath out slowly and raise a hand to lock it on Charlie's shoulder. "You're the man," I say. For the first time since he has joined us, I see him grin from one elfish ear to the other.

chapter nine

Herb and I finally agree on something: We'll paddle one more rapid before stopping for the night. Deep in the canyon here, the light is growing weak long before actual darkness is ready to set in, but the canyon is beginning to open up in places, allowing access to bits of land level enough that we can camp. I don't know how close we are to the falls, but I know I don't want to reach the lip too tired to pull off the quick ferry required to keep from spilling over. Anyway, there's no way we can complete a complicated portage around the falls before dark. Truth is, I'm pretty bushed. I figure that means Herb and Charlie are too. We've come a long way in high-stress conditions. Both Charlie and Herb have had close calls. I'm happy that I've done okay, but the long day has taken its toll.

"Just one more rapid," Herb is saying to Charlie. "Then we'll feed our faces and crash in the woods. Way to paddle all this way with your sleeping bag in a dry-bag in your boat. You're a real organized camper, you know, even if you shouldn't have come down the canyon. We'll get you out of here, don't you worry. But then it's straight back to camp with you. Your parents are probably having kittens."

Charlie doesn't respond. I wonder if Herb's or my parents are having kittens. I feel a surge of victory for having made mine worry. Or maybe they're just letting the camp handle it as they fit in a few more business appointments. If they ground me for this, I swear I'll run away from home for a lot longer. I've tasted freedom and tested my limits, and I'm getting stronger and prouder by the minute.

Of course, having Charlie along complicates my plan. Once we're on the lake, we'll be spotted and swooped down on for sure. If I can escape these two by then, Herb will do the job of turning Charlie over. Herb himself will be ready to go back by then, I figure. He's had his bit of fun. Anyway, from the sounds of his parents, they'll send the army to find their endangered son. I don't want the army after me.

Maybe I should sprint ahead in this

rapid, after all, and then lose them. Maybe I can get around the falls before dark. Without warning, I ferry out into the rapid, which looks like a big one.

"Hey!" Herb calls. "We're not ready!"

"Catch me if you can," I reply, but the thunder of the drop probably drowns out my message.

For a few minutes, I'm acing everything. My bow lifts and plunges through the big waves. My eyes are everywhere, sighting the rocks and reversals long before I'm near them. But I don't count on the one danger every river runner dreads: a submerged log. The bang as I hit it at full speed is sickening. Like a stone in a slingshot, I'm launched out of the canoe and into the drink before I can register a thing. Hours later, I'll reflect that I was lucky to be ricocheted beyond the log instead of sucked under it. All I know at the time is that my lungs are compressed almost to my backbone by the cold water. I'm gasping, I'm reaching, I'm being carried along by a coffin-shaped pocket of bubbles that turn strange, yellowy colors as my head bobs alternately on top of and then beneath the surface.

My lifejacket seems inadequate in this current. I fight to keep my face above water. I struggle to lift my feet, knowing that snagging them deep below me can mean a quick drowning. I reach my arms behind me and attempt to flutter kick toward the canyon walls, where quieter patches of water might give me a chance to climb out on a rock. It's a slow, terrifying process but better than being sucked further into midriver whirlpools that somersault me until I don't know which way is up or down. Every now and then my raised feet bump into a boulder. I bend my knees and spring off them like a frog, trying to work my way toward the canyon walls.

I feel my strength being sapped by the cold. My attempts to grab and hold onto climbable rock islands are slow and clumsy. Sluggishly, I lift my head to see what's coming up and feel adrenaline course through me like lightning. I'm heading fast into a log jammed across the water like a police barrier. It's right at water level. I know that where there are logs over water, there are typically branches beneath, ready to catch a stray swimmer like a fishnet. With every drop of strength I can command, I reach up as I'm hurtling into the log and hold on. I have nothing left in me to lift myself up onto it, but I refuse to surrender my hold and slip under it. My only chance is to hang on until Herb or Charlie can rescue me. What chance they have of positioning themselves to help me without joining me, I can't calculate. Not with my frozen brain.

I don't know how long I've held on, limbs locking slowly like a chicken tossed in a freezer, when I feel the log start moving. Why is it moving? my numbed mind asks. Then I see a pair of extra-small neoprene booties shuffling slowly toward me along the top of the log, like a tightrope walker's cautious feet. They stop far short of where I can reach up and clutch them. But they stop close enough that the small hands above them can toss me a rescue rope shaped into a lasso. Somehow, I understand that I'm to lift one hand at a time to let this circle fall over me and slip down to my waist. Somehow, I understand that I'm to maintain my icy grip a little longer, until the rope gets tied off and tightened. Then the feet come closer and a young face leans down into mine.

"Herb's coming," Charlie says. The log begins to shake like crazy, and I think of the folktale about the giant coming to roar at someone clinging to a bean-pole. *Fee-fi-fo-fum...* But this crawling giant and his pint-sized assistant grab me under my arms and shout at me to kick myself up on the log, which I do, or try to do.

Soon I'm lying on my stomach, cling-ing to the bark like a baby monkey clings to its mother's fur. I'm terrified of fall-ing back into the water, rope or not. But slowly, my coaches persuade me to crawl along to the safety of the cliff-side rock on which the log has wedged. Then they rip my wetsuit off, towel me down and force me to crawl into a sleeping bag. They feed me a chocolate bar and sips of water like a baby. I am glad they realize that my fingers are incapable of flexing at this point.

As I begin to come to my senses, I fumble for what I'm supposed to say.

"Thank you," I finally croak. I feel myself shaking. I am having difficulty forcing words from between my chattering teeth. "I'm sorry, really sorry. Stupid, really stupid. Won't take off on you again. Promise."

chapter ten

That night, I sleep like I've never slept in my life. We're in a patch of woods just beyond where the canyon has begun to open up. A bomb could have dropped beside me and I wouldn't have heard or felt it. When I do finally wake up, it's because Herb and Charlie are arguing.

"Yes, you are going to leave your kayak here," says Herb. "We can't take any chances of you going over the falls. You can paddle in the front of my canoe. You'll be safe there."

"You can't make me."

"Don't bet I can't make you. It's for your own good, you know, Charlie. Can't you see that you've been lucky up until now? We can't take on the responsibility when we know what's coming up."

"I'm as good as you guys. I've proven it."

I turn my head to see Charlie's arms crossed over his chest. Poor kid. Herb has been treating him like a toddler ever since he joined us. Not that I've done anything about it. I hate the little brat, don't I? But he deserves a break from Herb.

"Let him be," I say, sitting up.

"See?" Charlie says.

"You stay out of this, Wilf. We all know how much you've looked after Charlie on this trip."

"Oh yeah? You think I should manage him every second like you? Treat him like he has no skills or opinions of his own? Act like his nanny? Just give the kid a break, Herb."

"I will not give him a break if it means letting him hurt himself. No one else seems to be watching out for his safety."

Now it's Herb's arms crossed over his chest and Charlie looking from him to me.

"Herb," I repeat, "back off. Let him decide what he wants to paddle in. I'll watch out for him today, okay? He's sick to death of you and your 'coaching,' and I want some peace and quiet for once."

Herb looks from me to Charlie, undecided. "Okay," he says hesitantly. "It's about time you helped out with him." He stomps back to his canoe and begins packing.

Charlie smiles at me, but I turn my back on him and finger through what's left of our food supplies. At length, I

select my breakfast: canned peaches and
two slightly stale cinnamon buns. These
feel great in my belly as the three of us
slide our boats into the water and enjoy
a more leisurely set of rapids than we've
had for many miles.

"Nice part of the river," Herb observes
as he moves into the lead.

"Awesome," Charlie says as he surfs
a play wave and spins off it in show-off
fashion.

I'm supposed to keep Charlie between
Herb and me, but if he's going to stop
and play all the time, forget that. I pass
him and tail Herb, pretending I don't
hear Charlie when he calls out, "Wilf!
Look! A heron on shore."

The river grows ever gentler, as if
spent from its ride through the canyon.
Its deep green color allows me to see
almost to the bottom. I wish I had my
camera. I'm totally enjoying myself as I
slalom around obstacles and even put my

feet up on the bow thwart and stretch my hands behind my head on one particularly calm section.

But something tells me it's the calm before the storm. A few minutes later, my instincts are confirmed. The river speeds up, rounds a sharp bend and crescendos into a thunderous noise.

"Falls!" I scream as I see Herb dig deep for a pivot into the nearest eddy.

chapter eleven

Like dominoes touched by an invisible hand, we fall into one another in a tiny eddy, each reaching for dangling-root handholds on shore to ensure we don't get pulled back into the current.

I climb out first, forgetting to help Charlie as I haul my boat up. Herb shouts above the roar of the falls, "Way to help the kid, Wilf. You're useless."

Big deal. Charlie is doing fine climbing up the bank himself. He doesn't need Herb to hold out his hand for him. Once we're all on shore, we walk a few minutes until we reach the falls' edge and look down. They're impressive. Twenty-five feet down onto a pile of sharp rocks. Not much chance of anyone surviving if they went over, that's for sure. I shift my eyes to a steep, muddy path zigzagging down to the pool at the bottom. It's riddled with roots that might offer handholds but looks pretty marginal as a portage trail.

"Ropes," I shout to Charlie.

"I'm not letting him help us portage!" Herb shouts back, still competing with the sound of the falls. "Let him climb down first and wait for us. You and I can hand the boats down to one another on the ropes."

"Stop telling him what to do. Start asking him how *he* thinks he can help!" I yell.

"No, you let me organize the portage. You never do anything for that kid. I haven't seen you take one bit of responsibility for him today, so you're fired."

"Fired from what, you idiot?" I bellow, reaching out to grab him by his wetsuit's shoulder strap.

I don't know what Herb thinks I'm up to, but he lands me a hard punch in the chest. Soon we're sprawling on the rocky ground, fists flying, backs crunching into the path, mist from the falls washing our faces. It ends as fast as it starts, like both of us can't believe we're being so stupid. As we scramble up and brush ourselves off, we see an orange kayak slung on a shoulder moving toward us.

"He's trying to portage the kayak by himself!" Herb exclaims. Before either of us can run forward to help him, Charlie stumbles. The earth beneath him gives way, and he and his boat tumble down in a small landslide. They hit the water above the falls with a splash.

"Rescue rope!" I scream. I see Charlie failing in his efforts to regain shore. He's being sucked toward the waterfall. I reach the canoes first, grab the rescue rope and throw it as vigorously as I can. It misses Charlie by several feet. As I retrieve it frantically and coil it for a second throw, I see Charlie reaching out for a rock, clinging to it and pulling himself up on it.

"Attaboy," I mumble, but I'm horrified at how close he and his rock are to the edge of the falls.

Herb's hands are covering his mouth. He's speechless for once. "Our ropes aren't long enough," he finally says, sinking slowly to the ground.

"Not unless we tie them together," I say.

"Of course!" Herb leaps up. As he helps me finish pulling my rope in, he says, "Can you imagine how scared he must be?"

Ropes tied together now, I throw like I'm a major league pitcher in an over-time inning. Charlie, who appears to be trembling slightly, gives me a thumbs-up as he catches the other end. Herb moves to loop our end around a tree. I watch Charlie wrap his around his torso.

"Looks like he was paying attention during the knot-tying portion of sailing class," I say. "He's tying a bowline."

"And I've remembered to not tie mine off," Herb replies soberly. "The only safe thing to do is belay him. You pull while I take up the slack, okay?"

My fingers shake slightly as I clutch the rope and nod. It's going to take every-thing I have to pull him up against this current. "He has to hold the rope and his head up high enough that he planes above the water, or he'll drown while we're pulling him."

"Good thing he's so light-weight," Herb states.

We draw our breath collectively as Charlie steps to the edge of his rock and slowly lets himself back into the water. Now we pull like we're in the tug-o-war competition of our lives, which we are. Two strong camp seniors against one small junior and a roaring river. Slowly, he moves upstream toward us, stomach skimming the surface and head held high as we huff, puff and take in slack faster than champion fly fishermen with a record-breaking catch.

When Charlie is onshore, we take a few minutes to catch our breath. Then Herb crouches down to Charlie's height. "Charlie, this is my fault."

"Nope," I say, bending down awkwardly. "It's mine. I know you're an incredible, amazing kid—almost bionic—but I've been treating you like you're not a kid at all. I've been ignoring you, wishing I could get rid of you and Herb. This whole trip happened because that's how my parents treat me. I can't believe I'm doing that to a little kid."

Charlie looks at me curiously. "I'm not a little kid. You're the only one who lets me do stuff, Wilf."

Herb scratches his head. "I guess I'm being a control freak like my mom and dad."

Charlie grins. "You're not my parents. I don't need any stupid parents. I know how to kayak."

I laugh and place my hand on his helmet. "Oh, yes, you do need parents," I tell him. "So, now that your kayak has found its own way down the falls, tell us: Do you want to scramble down and untie the canoes as they come to you or stay up top and help lower them?"

Charlie smirks. "I'm helping Wilf. Are you up or down, Wilf?"

Herb laughs. "Of course. I'll go down

first, then. Better keep my helmet and lifejacket on in case you two let go before you're supposed to."

chapter twelve

It takes forever to lower the canoes down on ropes. Even if Charlie is strong for a ten-year-old, I sure could use Herb's muscle to help lower them. But Charlie loves every minute of being my helper. And much as I hate to admit it, I'm kind of taking a shine to the kid. Yeah, he's a pain, but then so am I, eh? In fact, he's way too much like me. Stubborn, competitive, adventurous, no fear and lots of attitude. I feel sorry for his parents.

So now we're launching, and guess who insists on riding in my canoe, since we seem to be one kayak short? Good thing I brought a spare paddle. Did the kayak and its paddle get swallowed by the waterfalls? I doubt it. That little orange play boat is just doing the solo trip I'd planned on doing. But I'm having too much fun to be jealous of it. Yeah, fun. In a totally weird family of three.

It helps that we're done with the really hairy stuff. At least, I hope. So far, the first few rapids after the waterfall are hardly rapids at all. They're perfect for someone like Charlie, even if he thinks he's too good for them now.

"Hey buddy, pretend that orange-colored rock over there is the finish line of a race. Show me your best sprint."

Whoa. That's all it takes to fire up my new partner. It's like setting off a rocket booster. I can hang out in the stern with my feet up on the thwarts, head back. He doesn't even know it. I just stick my paddle in when he looks back or needs a little ruddering.

But as it turns out, the orange rock isn't an orange rock at all. It's his water-logged kayak plastered against a rock. We all pile out and, working together as a team, finally extract it.

"Can't blame it for hugging that rock after what it has gone through," Herb jokes. "Good thing it's plastic."

Indeed, there's hardly a scratch on it.

"Think I could have gone over the falls in it and lived?" Charlie asks, inspecting it.

"Don't even think about it," Herb and I say together.

"Hey! Is that my paddle?" he asks, pointing to an eddy further downstream.

Herb canoes down to it, picks it up, gives us a victory sign.

Too bad, I think. Now I've lost my slave. So Charlie climbs back in his kayak, and the three of us meander on down through playful rapids: canoe, kayak and canoe, staying in the order we've agreed on. Herb and I are careful to pick routes Charlie can follow, more careful than we were above. Even if it's easier here, there's no point losing him after all we've been through. And okay, I've undergone an attitude adjustment.

"Hey Herb. The way the trees look up ahead, I'd say we're about to dump into a lake. You figure?"

He slows his stroke rate for a second. "Yeah, maybe."

"Then what?"

"Well, first we break out the marsh-mallows, because I've been saving them for a celebration. Then you catch us a fish and we'll have a delicious fry-up. Then we look for a break in the trees that might be a road access."

"Then you and Charlie can hike out if no one has shown up looking for us yet."

"You're still set on staying here?"

"Can I stay with you?" Charlie asks.

"Not in a month of Sundays, kid. You get back to camp and show Patrick and Claire how your ferry moves and eddy turns have improved."

"Awwww!"

"Not much food left, Wilf," Herb objects.

"That's what my fish hooks and survival skills are for. Tell 'em I'll be back before my two weeks is up."

"They'll grill Charlie and me about where you are."

"Well, I know Charlie won't break," I tease back.

As we're talking, the river gets shallow and gurgles as it feeds into the lake.

"Sounds like it's farting," Charlie says, laughing so hard his kayak shakes.

"It's just saying goodbye."

chapter thirteen

We take a good look around. Forget a break in the trees indicating a road. The glare of the sun on a bunch of vehicles beside a dirt ramp across the lake hits us. It's matched by the sparkle of aluminum canoes coming at us, like maybe someone's binoculars spotted us on the last portion of the river and served as the signal for launching.

"Three double canoes. Isn't that a bit large for a Camp Wild posse?" Herb says uncertainly. "I think we might be in a little trouble when they get here."

"Doesn't leave many canoes back at camp," I mumble, realizing I have no time to hide now.

"Or counselors," Charlie inserts.

We paddle slowly toward the middle of the lake as the canoes close on us. I can't figure out who's in the boats. I'm guessing it might be Claire and Patrick in the front one, and judging from the color of their clothing, park rangers in the second. Looks like a middle-aged couple in the third. Herb's folks? The couple is struggling to keep up with the other two boats, like they're not very fit, but their paddling technique clearly shows they've spent lots of time in canoes. Hopefully they're not police officers or anything.

My paddle keeps dipping, my eyes on the party approaching. Definitely Patrick and Claire, definitely rangers. But...*my* mom and dad? What the heck would they be doing here, in a canoe of all things?

As five canoes and one kayak converge in the middle of the lake, people practically tip over reaching out to shake hands or, in the case of Mom and Dad, hug me.

"We're so relieved you're safe," Claire gushes. "I just want you to know how happy we are that you're all here. Everyone at camp has been worrying like crazy about the three of you. Especially you, Charlie," she says as he squirms a little and gives me a sideways smile.

"Herb, your parents are at Camp Wild now, manning the phones. Charlie, your parents are a mess."

"Before you say a word," Dad starts—not knowing I'm incapable of saying a word as I stare at him and Mom in utter shock—"your mother and I want to say we're very angry you would dare to try a stunt like this. What is it you were trying to prove, young man?"

Slowly my tongue comes unstuck. "I told you that you couldn't force me to go to summer camp," I say as defiantly as I can.

Claire starts staring at the water. The others are trying not to shift in their canoe seats.

My parents both start speaking at once, until my mother puts her hand on my dad's shoulder as if insisting she get her turn first. "You had us worried sick," she starts. "Did you think about how panicked we'd be? And why put others in danger, especially someone as young as this boy?"

Charlie bristles at that but seems to know when to keep silent.

"They followed me," I declare. "I didn't put anyone up to anything. I didn't want anything to do with them. Just ask them."

Dad looks from Charlie to Herb and seems satisfied with the looks they return.

"Actually," I add boldly, "I didn't think you'd worry much at all. I thought I'd get the summer I really wanted, and you'd just fit in some more work. You know, take care of clients." The word "work" comes out way louder and more bitter than I plan. It also seems to hit and stick in them like a carelessly tossed fishhook.

Dad opens his mouth, then closes it, just like a new catch in the bottom of the boat. He also goes a bit red.

"So," he finally begins, as Patrick trails his canoe paddle in the water and sneaks glances at the rangers, "you thought you were too old for Camp Wild, and you thought you had to do something dangerous to make your point."

"Sweetie, I think you're ignoring his real point," my mom says unexpectedly.

"Which is?" my father says stubbornly.

She gives him the silent treatment.

"That you kind of dumped him at camp," Herb ventures.

Everyone turns and stares at Herb. Charlie gets an evil smirk on his face.

"'Cause you work too much!" Charlie explodes, taking his cue from Herb's remark. "And he's way more adventurous than you are!"

Claire reaches across to put her hand over Charlie's mouth. She removes it right away, but he gets the idea.

"Is that what you think?" Dad asks, but his tone has lost its sharp edge.

I shrug. "Whatever."

"You know," my mother speaks up, "we used to canoe and camp a lot before you were born." My dumbstruck look seems to amuse her. "It has been a long time. And I guess we've been working way too much. But believe it or not, we can understand why you might want to do something more adventurous. I guess we didn't listen very well when you tried to tell us that."

"This was a very foolish way to try and get your way," Dad says, gesturing toward the river behind us. He takes a deep breath. "But here we are. And you know what? Except for the worry and anger, I kind of enjoyed the trip out here. I'd forgotten how beautiful this lake is." He studies me, and his voice goes softer. "What do you say we stay on a few days, roast some marshmallows, get some mosquito bites, do some hiking and canoeing together?" He coughs. "The bank will run itself for a few days. And maybe your mother can make a few calls from camp and arrange for a break. Somehow I'm guessing Camp Wild would be okay with dismissing you early."

Patrick and Claire look up, then at one another.

"I'm sure it can be arranged," Patrick says, squinting at me a little.

I try clearing my throat, but that's about all I can manage.

"Luck-eeeee," Charlie protests. "You're going to make me go back, aren't you?" he accuses Claire and Patrick.

"Absolutely. No question," Patrick responds sternly, shaking his head while trying not to smile. The rangers look far less amused. I'm guessing that they're still waiting their turn for a nasty lecture.

"But if you survived the canyon, Charlie, I reckon you can help teach the other juniors," Claire adds. "Can I count on you as a helper?"

Charlie looks at me and shrugs. "Dunno. I don't really like kids."

This sets us all off laughing, even the rangers, which breaks the tension still hanging at the edges of our reunion.

"Wilf, we promise we won't make you go to Camp Wild next year," Dad says solemnly.

I look at Herb and Charlie, then at Claire.

"But I'd like to come back next year," I announce. "Then Claire could train me up as a junior counselor."

Patrick looks startled, then angry, like I might have to submit to a few severe lectures and suffer a period of probation between now and then.

Herb says, "Me too."

"All right!" Charlie explodes, jabbing his kayak paddle up and down wildly.

Claire gives me a glowing smile that makes me think I'm going to capsize in my canoe right then and there and need a deep-water rescue if not mouth-to-mouth resuscitation.

Pam Withers is author of *Raging River*, *Peak Survival*, *Adrenalin Ride* and *Skater Stuntboys*. She is also a former summer camp coordinator, whitewater kayak instructor and river raft guide. She lives in Vancouver with her husband and teenage son when not touring North America giving school presentations. Her website is www.TakeItToTheXtreme.com.

Also in the Orca Currents series

Queen of the Toilet Bowl
by Frieda Wishinsky

"Ohmygod! Is that what it said?"

I wondered what they were whispering about. I knew something was going on but what?

A crowd was milling around the lockers, talking and laughing, but as soon as I showed up, the noise stopped dead.

A few kids coughed. A few others snapped their lockers shut and left. One girl gave me a strange look, as if I had horns growing out of my head.

When Renata is chosen to play the lead role in the school musical, students who used to ignore her start saying hello and congratulating her in the hall. She is happy until it becomes evident that Karin, a wealthy girl who expected to get the lead role, will go to great lengths to ruin Renata's reputation.